WELCOME TO HOLYROOD PARK

This is a unique place, full of recreational opportunities, rich in history and prehistory, and important for wildlife. Now at the heart of Scotland's capital city, this area has been used and occupied by people for thousands of years.

But this striking landscape can be traced back far beyond that, to volcanic activity 340 million years ago. The rocky slopes formed then – and reshaped over millennia – have attracted generation after generation of geologists.

The Park's rugged nature provides varied habitats for many plants and animals, some very rare.

It has seen farming and fort-building, hunting and worship, army encampments and royal pageantry, warfare and ritual, murder and mystery. Its geology, archaeology, history and wildlife make it a place of extraordinary significance and fragility, to be cherished and conserved for future visitors.

So important and so fragile are the Park and its archaeology that it is designated as a Scheduled Monument of national importance. As such, it is one of Scotland's legally protected places, managed by Historic Environment Scotland according to the Holyrood Park Regulations.

CONTENTS

Illustrative map	2	A new abbey	16	Explore Holyrood Park	36
		Stewart royalty at Holyrood	18	A year-round wildlife habitat	38
About Holyrood Park	4	A royal park	20	Meadow and grassland plants	40
How the Park was formed	6	A debtors' sanctuary	21	Rock and scree plants	42
Rocks of many kinds	8	An age of violence and change	22	Aquatic plants	44
Traces in stone: Mesolithic and Neolithic Holyrood	10	Discovery and progress	24	Invertebrates	45
New ways to live and work: the Bronze Age	11	Winter sports	26	Mammals and amphibians	46
		Buried secrets	28	Birds	47
Enclosures, hillforts and invasion: the Iron Age and Romans	12	The Queen's Park	29	Historic buildings and structures: Holyrood Abbey and Palace	50
		In peacetime and in war	30		
Working the land	14	Park life	32	Historic buildings and structures: in and around the Park	52
		Holyrood Park in fiction and on film	34	Historic buildings and structures: Duddingston	54
				Help us protect the Park	56
				Acknowledgements and credits	57

Cover. A view from Arthur's Seat over Salisbury Crags and the city.

Above. Bronze Age axe heads found in the Park.

FIND YOUR WAY AROUND HOLYROOD PARK

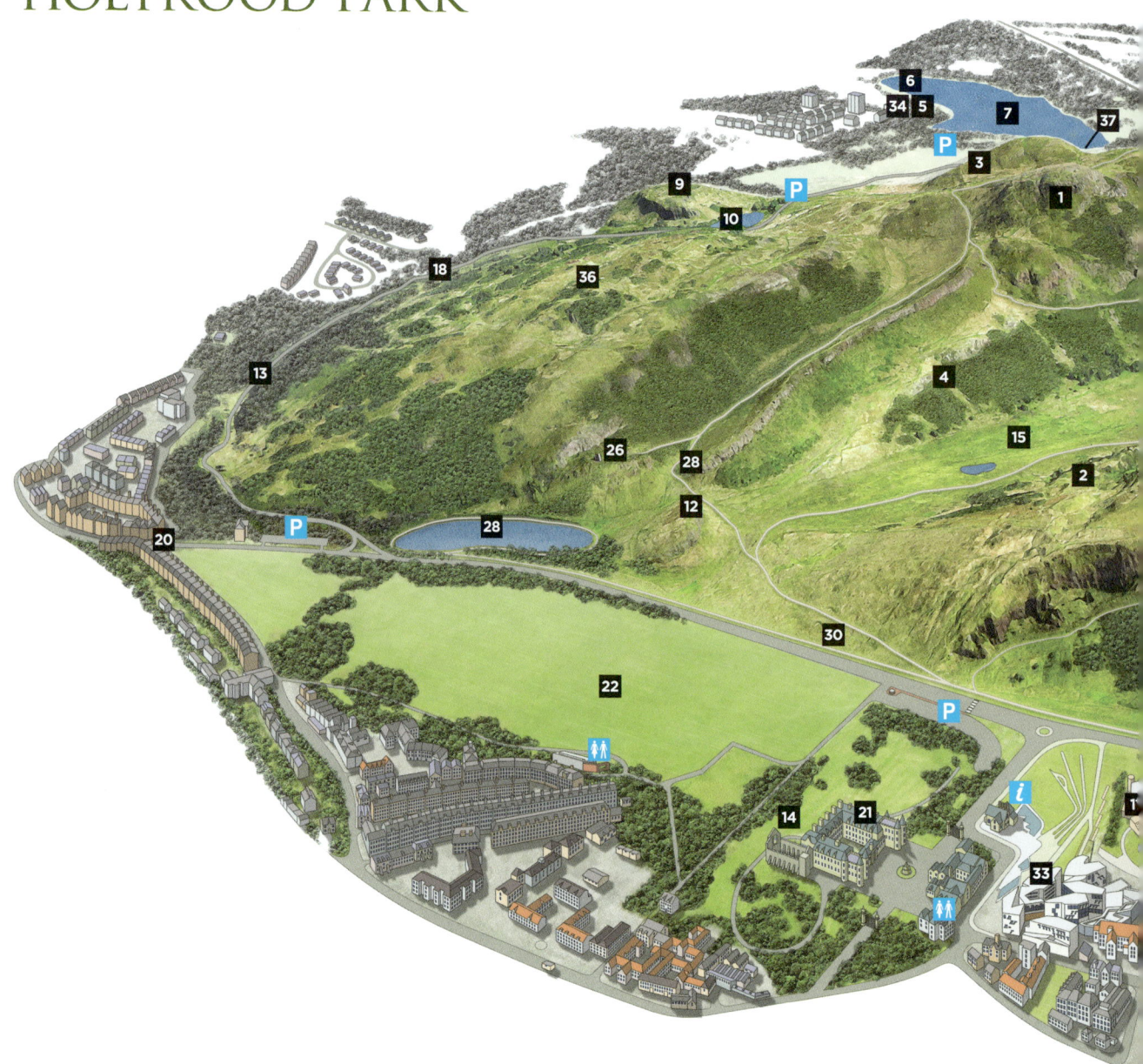

Holyrood Park Ranger Service
Our Rangers help to manage and conserve the Park, and assist visitors in enjoying and understanding it. They also offer regular guided walks and deliver educational activities. Contact them for further information:
0131 652 8150 or rangers@hes.scot

P Car parking
Parking is free except at Queen's Drive adjacent to the Palace of Holyroodhouse. Parking at Dunsapie Loch is only available at certain times.

Illustrative Map

Points of interest/Facilities

1. Arthur's Seat
2. Camstane Quarry
3. Crow Hill
4. The Dasses
5. Dr Neil's Garden
6. Duddingston Kirk
7. Duddingston Loch
8. Dumbiedykes
9. Dunsapie Crag
10. Dunsapie Loch
11. Dynamic Earth
12. Haggis Knowe
13. High Road (Queen's Drive)
14. Holyrood Abbey
15. Hunter's Bog
16. Hutton's Section
17. Innocent Railway
18. Lily Hill
19. Murder Acre
20. Muschat's Cairn
21. Palace of Holyroodhouse
22. Playing Fields (Parade Ground)
23. Powderhouse Brae
24. Radical Road
    Please refer to our website for the latest information on path closures and access.
25. Raven's Rock
26. St Anthony's Chapel
27. St Leonard's Crag
28. St Anthony's Well
29. St Margaret's Loch
30. St Margaret's Well
31. Salisbury Crags
32. Samson's Ribs
33. Scottish Parliament
34. Thomson's Tower
35. Wells o' Wearie
36. Whinny Hill
37. Windy Gowl

i Visitor Centre
P Parking
Toilets

ABOUT HOLYROOD PARK

Holyrood Park has a very long history and prehistory. This is fitting, because it was here, in the late 1700s, that James Hutton discovered proof that the Earth was very much older than previously believed. In doing so he gave birth to modern geology – the scientific study of rock formations and landscapes.

About Holyrood Park 5

In the pages that follow, you can read about the Park's geological origins, and about the human activity that came later. People have been using and inhabiting this landscape for about 10,000 years, and many have left their mark.

Over those many centuries, they have used its crags, slopes and glens in a wide variety of ways: to farm, hunt, defend themselves, worship and engage in many leisure pursuits. This is their story, and the story of a unique and protected place.

Below. A view of the Park from the north-east, with St Margaret's Loch in the foreground.

HOW THE PARK WAS FORMED

At the start of the Carboniferous Period, 360 million years ago, the Park was a swampy, low-lying area close to the sea, located just south of the Equator. Since then, much has changed.

1 360 million years ago
The area slowly subsided and filled with sediment – pebbles, sand and mud – washed from the mountains to the north. A thick layer of sedimentary rock formed the bedrock that now underlies much of Edinburgh. It has provided the city with building stone, coal, ironstone and lime.

2 3 342 million years ago
The landscape was suddenly changed by an eruption of the small but complex volcano we now call Arthur's Seat. This and subsequent events have left us with varied rock types and a spectacular landscape of cliffs, craggy summits and grassy valleys.

Below. Volcanic rock.

Arthur's Seat was one of many small volcanoes erupting on this flat coastal plain, creating tough igneous rocks, very different from the layers of sedimentary rock. These volcanoes were scattered all over central Scotland, and formed most of the high landmarks of the Lothians and Fife.

These were basaltic volcanoes, fed by magma rising from deep underground. They erupted red-hot lava that spilled out of craters and spread across the landscape. The lava cooled quickly, hardening to black basalt full of gas bubbles. Over time, basalt layers built up, forming low cones that rose a few hundred metres above the plain.

Sometimes the magma interacted with water, turning it instantly to steam. This caused rapid expansion, forcing a hot, gassy magma mix to the surface, where it exploded in clouds of black ash and flying lava blocks. This dramatic volcanic activity accounts for the rough red rock on the high slopes of Arthur's Seat.

But volcanoes don't last forever. Eventually the pulse of rising magma slowed and stopped, and the magma solidified. All was quiet, and the accumulation of sedimentary rock buried the volcano.

4 335 million years ago
More magma forced its way towards the surface, but this time there was no volcanic eruption. Instead, the magma got trapped underground, forced sideways through existing rock layers, and cooled slowly to form the tough, crystalline igneous rock called dolerite that forms Salisbury Crags. Sedimentary rocks continued to build up above the volcano, and at times a shallow sea covered the entire area.

5 300 million–2 million years ago
Movements of the tectonic plates that make up the Earth's surface lifted up these rocks, and the layers were tilted to the east. This began a process of slow erosion, stripping away hundreds of metres of overlying rock. As Europe drifted northwards, away from the Equator, Arthur's Seat and Salisbury Crags slowly rose towards the surface.

6 7 Over the past 2 million years
Ice sheets as much as 1 mile (1.8km) thick advanced from the west, grinding away the softer layers, and exposing today's crags and cliffs **8**. They left behind the varied topography of volcanic hills and flat, swampy lowlands that the first humans discovered a mere 10,000 years ago.

How the Park was formed 7

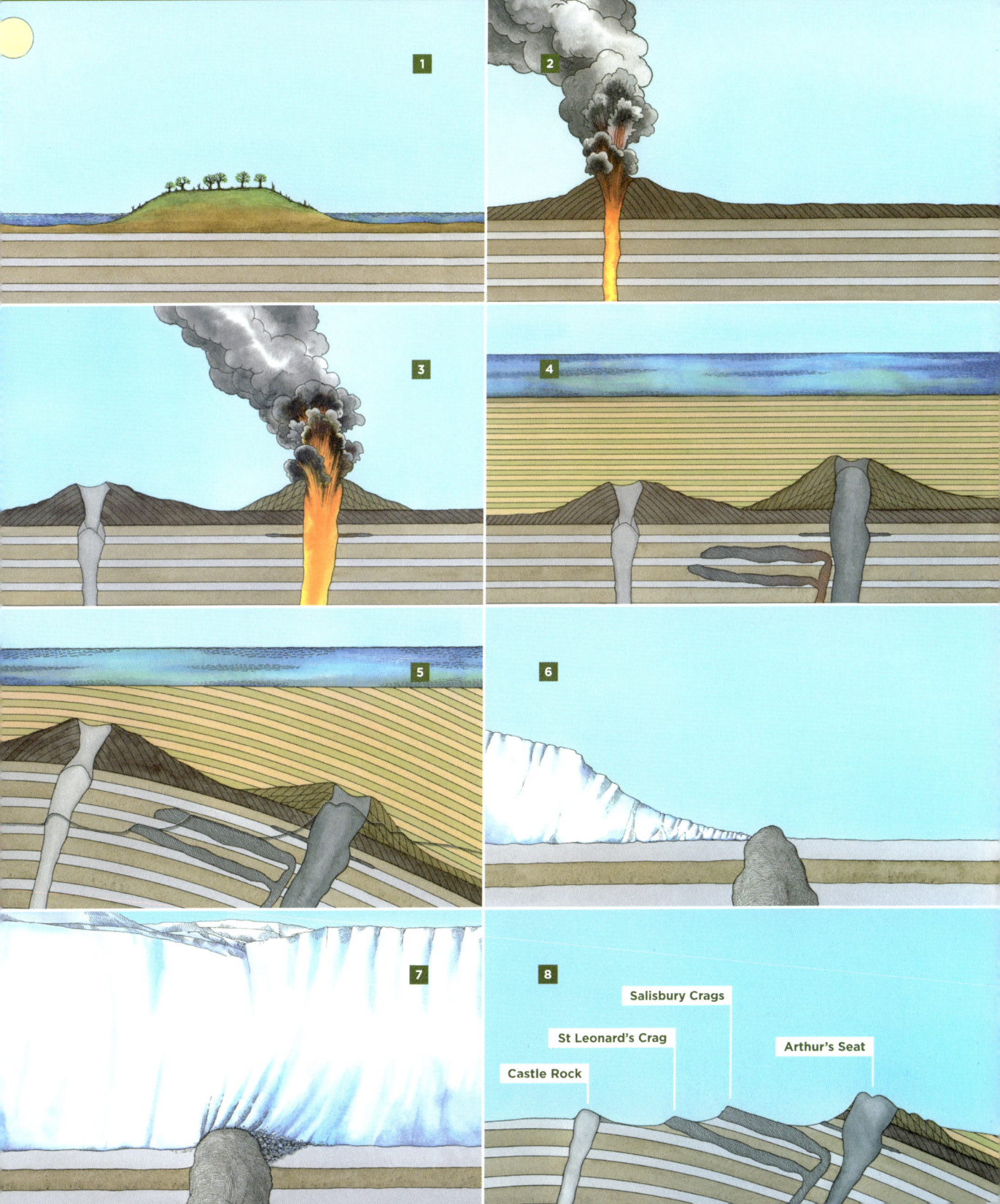

ROCKS OF MANY KINDS

The varied geological story of the Park has left us with a jumble of different rock types. This is part of the attraction for visitors and local users today, and the complex landscape provides the basis for a variety of wildlife habitats.

1 Sandstone

The oldest rocks in the Park are layers of sandstone and other sedimentary rocks. They are exposed in the Camstane Quarry close to Salisbury Crags, and in places underneath the Crags themselves.

Often coloured pink, sandstone contains clues to the environment where it was formed. Fossilised ripples and mud-cracks indicate a wet environment that sometimes dried out. The sandstone layers quarried at Camstane did not yield high-quality building stone, as the rock is coarse, quite soft and full of imperfections.

2 Basalt

Whinny Hill is formed of a stack of basalt lava flows – the eroded cone of the Arthur's Seat volcano. Look out for gas bubbles, and softer layers between the lavas that have been worn away to leave small valleys. Blocks of basalt make up the main building stone for St Anthony's Chapel – but note the sandstone blocks around the doors and windows. These were easier to carve.

3 Agglomerate – crater rock

The centre of the volcano is made mostly of a rough, red rock full of fragments of lava. This is agglomerate, which filled the crater of the volcano. Blocks of lava and other rocks are encased in fine, red ash. This rock was formed when loose fragments blasted into the air during eruptions fell back into the volcanic vent and consolidated.

4 Tuff – volcanic ash

This soft rock is difficult to find in the Park, but it formed in areas where volcanic ash blew in the wind and piled up on the slopes of the volcano. Sometimes the iron content of this rock is unoxidised, giving a light green colour. Look for some blocks of tuff in the walls of St Anthony's Chapel.

5 Dolerite

This is the toughest rock in the Park, and forms the dramatic cliff of Salisbury Crags. Originally this was a dense, black, crystalline rock that formed deep below ground, and has only recently been exposed to the elements.

Over time, the surface becomes weathered to an attractive rusty red colour. Like most igneous rocks, dolerite is full of cracks, which let the water in. Freezing and thawing break it up, so rock falls are common under the cliffs of Salisbury Crags.

1

Rocks of many kinds

TRACES IN STONE: MESOLITHIC AND NEOLITHIC HOLYROOD

The Park may appear to be wild, rugged and untouched, but the landscape you see today is the result of thousands of years of human activity.

The earliest evidence of people in the Park dates from around 7,000 to 8,000 years ago, in a period known as the Mesolithic (Mid-Stone Age). The landscape would then have been much more wooded, with boggy valleys and small lochs in the lowest-lying ground.

Mesolithic people made use of the rich natural resources for fishing, fowling and hunting. There is no evidence that they settled here, but stone tools such as a flint flake found on Whinny Hill show that they passed through.

Early agriculture

Around 6,000 years ago, at the dawn of the Neolithic (New Stone Age), the first farming communities began to settle and work the land. These earliest settlers again left little trace, but we can imagine how the Park's appearance would have begun to change, as woodland was cleared for growing crops and rearing livestock.

Again, stone tools provide our only evidence for these earliest settlers. Examples include a flint arrowhead and scraper found close to the summit of Arthur's Seat, and a stone axe near Duddingston Kirk.

DEATH DUTIES

Prehistoric burial sites have been discovered in the Park, revealing the funeral rites practised here. At Windy Gowl near Duddingston Loch, an urn containing cremated human remains was found inside a cist or stone coffin. Another cist was buried close by. These suggest rituals typical of Bronze Age Scotland.

Right and above. Simple flint tools and arrowheads of Neolithic date found in the Park.

NEW WAYS TO LIVE AND WORK: THE BRONZE AGE

It was not until the Bronze Age, starting around 2000 BC, that people really began to leave their mark on this landscape.

The most striking suggestion of Bronze Age activity is on the south-eastern flank of Arthur's Seat, which is skirted by over a dozen cultivation terraces – strips of levelled ground for growing crops. Some of these may date from this period.

At this time, farming communities lived and worked in small, unenclosed groups of houses. Six faint indentations on The Dasses have been very tentatively identified as a row of roundhouses. But despite these tantalising traces, there is no substantial evidence of Bronze Age dwellings in the Park.

Below. A Bronze Age axehead found on Dunsapie Crag.

GLIMMERS OF METAL

Numerous metal artefacts – and objects related to metalworking – have been discovered in the Park. Most of them date to the Late Bronze Age and Iron Age.

The most impressive discovery is the Duddingston Hoard: almost 50 metal objects discovered while dredging the loch in 1778. It included spearheads, swords, a cauldron handle and a rapier, and remains one of the largest Bronze Age metalwork assemblages found in Scotland.

Many of the objects were broken, and they were once thought to be scrap pieces kept aside for re-use.

However, they had been deliberately broken and carefully deposited, possibly during a ceremony to end their use. Bronze Age and Iron Age rituals are known to have included offerings of metal objects in watery places.

Elsewhere in the Park, swords, axes and moulds for casting metal objects have been found. Two bronze axe-heads were discovered on Dunsapie Crag, and two bronze swords were found during the construction of Queen's Drive. The swords are high quality, suggesting that the owners were powerful individuals, who had access to either trade routes or skilled craftsmen.

The hoard is now held by National Museums Scotland in Edinburgh.

Above. The hoard of metal weapons and tools found in Duddingston Loch in 1778.

ENCLOSURES, HILLFORTS AND INVASION: THE IRON AGE AND ROMANS

In southern Scotland, people began working with iron around 500 BC. As this new Iron Age began, there was also a growth in population, agriculture and settlement.

Towards the middle of the Iron Age, people began to create enclosed settlements – single homesteads, villages and hillforts. Walls of stone, earth or timber were built around these sites, defining the territory, providing protection and perhaps controlling animals.

The hillforts that appeared during this period hint at an increasingly complex society, with growing competition for land and resources and a desire to demonstrate power and wealth.

At least four hillforts were built in Holyrood Park, taking advantage of natural defences such as rocky outcrops and terraces – though they were probably not all in use at the same time.

There were also hillforts on the surrounding summits, including Castle Rock (now the site of Edinburgh Castle).

A strong position
The Park was a strategically important location, where powerful people lived, and communities gathered or sought refuge.

During the 1st millennium AD, what is now Edinburgh lay at the edge of a frontier land, contested over by different regional groups. Arthur's Seat and Salisbury Crags provided vantage points from which to see and be seen.

Probably the earliest of the Park's hillforts, and also the largest, was on Salisbury Crags. It was enclosed by a long, low bank which still runs along the west slope of Hunter's Bog. Built with a stone base, it was probably topped by a palisade of timber stakes. It is thought to date between 500 and 100 BC, and may have contained houses and other structures.

Below. Dunsapie Crag hillfort as it may have looked when in use.

The Iron Age and Romans

Downsizing

The fort crowning Dunsapie Crag was smaller still but more elaborate, and now offers some of the best evidence of Iron Age settlement in the Park. The hilltop is surrounded by banks built from earth and stone; and the interior has traces of circular platforms where timber roundhouses probably stood.

Stone moulds found here indicate metalworking, and middens (rubbish heaps) provide evidence of domestic life.

The next largest fort was on Arthur's Seat itself. The remains of two low, stony banks can be traced on the eastern slopes, running across Crow Hill towards Arthur's Seat. These defended it from attack via the easiest approach.

There was also a small fort on Samson's Ribs. It may have enclosed a number of roundhouses.

These structures may not have been built to last. The fort on Salisbury Crags has a largely featureless interior, and may only have been occupied seasonally. Perhaps it served as a regional meeting place.

None of the hillforts seem to have been occupied for very long. They may have been abandoned in favour of other sites such as Castle Rock, which provided more suitable terrain.

Little survives of the hillforts now, but they were once imposing features in the landscape, visible for miles around.

The Roman era

Roman forces advanced into Scotland in the 70s and 80s AD, and although the occupation was sporadic, Roman power and influence continued in the area until around 400 AD.

There is little evidence of Roman activity within the Park, but small items such as coins provide clues of trade and interaction between the invaders and native tribes.

A Roman ring was found at the Samson's Ribs hillfort site in 1969. It has been dated to the 1st century BC, but was probably brought here more than a century later, perhaps owned by a Roman soldier.

By the time the Romans departed, Edinburgh had become an important centre, with a high-status settlement on Castle Rock.

FARMED OUT

Slightly east of Dunsapie Crag was a small farmstead, built in a hollow scooped into the hillside. It was connected to the fort by an outlying rampart, though is probably later in date. It would have contained one or more timber roundhouses and other structures such as barns or byres.

Above left. A stone mould found in the Park, that was used in metalwork.

Above right. A Roman ring, probably brought to Scotland by a Roman soldier; a Roman coin of the 2nd century AD. Both were found in the Park.

WORKING THE LAND

People began to shape the Park from as early as the Mesolithic era, around 6,500 years ago. We do not know exactly when the first homes were established here, but the whole landscape was used for farming from the Bronze Age. It has continued in some form almost to the present day.

The cultivation terraces near Dunsapie Loch probably date from as far back as the Bronze Age. Later developments can also be seen. Encroaching into the early terraces is a furlong of rig-and-furrow – a corrugated pattern created by medieval farming.

The best-preserved rig-and-furrow can be seen just below the road at Powderhouse Brae. Similar marks are also visible on the back of Salisbury Crags, sloping down to Hunter's Bog. They are best seen at dusk, illuminated by a low sun.

We cannot be sure what was grown in the Park, but evidence from historical records and archaeological investigations points to cereal crops such as barley, oats, wheat and rye. Flax – for oil or cloth – and fodder crops may also have been grown.

Beasts of the field

The Park was also used for grazing from early times. Monks of Kelso and Holyrood Abbeys almost certainly kept sheep here. On the third-highest terrace of the Dasses there are traces of a yard, byre and cottage. These are probably the remains of a post-medieval shepherd's cottage.

Following the creation of a royal park in 1541, the land was largely reserved for grazing cattle and sheep to stock royal kitchens.

After the early 1600s livestock farming became dominant. The parkland was profitable, providing hay, veal, wool, lamb, and rabbits. It was divided into different zones for grazing, which were leased to tenants.

Banks and enclosures survive across the Park, especially concentrated on Whinny Hill. Their age is uncertain, but they were probably used to contain livestock. Grazing continued in the Park until 1977.

Left. The cultivation terraces as they may have looked in medieval times.

Above. The cultivation terraces above Dunsapie Loch.

Right. Agricultural workers depicted in a manuscript of about 1330.

A NEW ABBEY

The first major event in Holyrood's medieval history was the foundation of the abbey. This was an act of thanksgiving in 1128 by the pious King David I.

According to legend, David was out hunting when he was charged by a stag, which gored him in the thigh. David held up his hands to defend himself, and found he was holding a rood (or crucifix). When it touched the stag's antlers, the animal disappeared.

The crucifix was said to contain a fragment of the True Cross – the actual cross on which Jesus died. This revered relic, known as the Black Rood, had been brought to Edinburgh by David's mother, Queen Margaret (later St Margaret), and was perhaps the most important religious artefact in medieval Scotland. It was seized by Edward I of England, after his successful invasion in 1296.

The abbey was founded for the Augustinian order. This was probably due to the influence of Robert, Bishop of St Andrews, and former leader of the Augustinian priory at Scone. The Augustinian canons of Holyrood were given permission to found a burgh, the Canongate, which remained a separate authority from the city of Edinburgh until the 1800s, and still has the same name.

Although founded for spiritual purposes, Holyrood Abbey was often put to secular use. Early meetings of the colloquium (the forerunner of parliament) were held at the abbey in the later 1200s.

HOLY LAND

Bronze Age burials and ritual deposits in the Park suggest it had long-standing religious significance, possibly associated with its natural springs. The people in this area adopted Christianity around 500–700 AD, and there may have been a church establishment at Holyrood long before the abbey, which may have been founded on a pre-existing religious site.

Below. The ruins of Holyrood Abbey, just outside the Park in the grounds of the royal palace.

A new abbey

Right. David II and his English wife Joan as depicted in the Forman Armorial around 1560.

Below right. A statue of Robert the Bruce at Stirling Castle.

THE AUGUSTINIANS

The men who came to live at Holyrood Abbey were canons of the Augustinian order. These were priests who lived communally at the abbey, but might leave it to preach in the surrounding area. They lived according to a code of faith and conduct known as St Augustine's Rule.

Augustinians were known for the hospitality they offered to monarchs and their guests, and were not required to stay in their monasteries, which enabled them to work in administrative roles for the crown. This may explain why the abbey was founded so close to Edinburgh Castle, an important royal residence.

Above. St Augustine depicted in a medieval manuscript.

Bruce at Holyrood

In 1328, King Robert the Bruce held a parliament at Holyrood, during which the Treaty of Edinburgh was ratified. This agreement brought a temporary halt to the Wars of Independence between Scotland and England.

Its terms included the marriage of Bruce's son – later David II – to Joan, sister of Edward III of England. It also brought English recognition, previously withheld, of Bruce as the rightful king of Scots. The treaty also included the return of the Black Rood to Scotland (though it was seized again by the English in 1346).

Bruce stayed at Holyrood during the parliament: by this time there was a royal residence within the abbey, though it was probably modest in scale.

David II's decision to be buried at Holyrood, rather than alongside his father at Dunfermline, suggests a growing royal attachment to the site. Over time, the royal residence developed into the Palace of Holyroodhouse.

STEWART ROYALTY AT HOLYROOD

As Edinburgh gained importance as a royal centre, the guesthouse at Holyrood Abbey grew to become a grand royal palace.

The early Stewart kings, Robert II and Robert III, generally preferred to stay in their traditional power bases in the south and west. Holyrood perhaps held bad associations for Robert II, for it was here, at a general council of 1384, that he was removed from power. Control was given to his heir, the Earl of Carrick (later Robert III), who became guardian of the kingdom.

Damage to the abbey caused by the English invasion of 1385 may also have diminished Holyrood's appeal for the Stewart kings. But throughout the 1400s it developed as a favoured residence and a location for court ceremony.

James I chose Holyrood in 1429 as the location for the formal submission of Alexander, Lord of the Isles, effective ruler of much of western Scotland. Alexander, 'clad only in shirt and drawers and on his knees', surrendered to James before the high altar of the abbey. After a stage-managed intercession by James's wife, Queen Joan, Alexander was imprisoned at Tantallon Castle, 25 miles to the east.

The following year, Joan gave birth to the future James II. This James went on to be crowned, married and buried in the abbey church.

A glittering palace

By the early 1500s, Holyrood's royal status was firmly established. It was under James IV that it took on a separate identity as 'the place and palace of Halirudehous'.

A herald who attended the marriage of James IV to Margaret Tudor described the palace as richly furnished. It was probably this marriage that prompted James to begin transforming the building, to provide suitable lodgings for his English bride. His son James V also carried out extensive work at the palace and even installed a menagerie of exotic beasts, including a lion and two bears.

Above. James IV and Margaret Tudor. Their wedding in 1503 may have prompted the development of Holyrood Palace.

The queen's house

Holyrood became the primary residence of James V's daughter, Mary Queen of Scots, when she returned from France in 1561 to reign in person.

It was here that she married her second and third husbands, Lord Darnley and the Earl of Bothwell.

Mary's time here was frequently turbulent. In her first week at Holyrood, she attended Mass, having gained special permission to continue this Catholic practice in the newly Protestant country. However, her worship was interrupted by a group of Protestants. They caused a disturbance in the courtyard, calling for the priest to be murdered.

When murder did take place here in March 1566, the victim was Mary's private secretary. David Rizzio had been painted as a dangerous influence on the queen by a group of conspirators who had lost power at court. Aided by Darnley, with whom the queen was at odds, assassins burst into Mary's private chambers. Led by Lord Ruthven, who wore a suit of armour for the occasion, they stabbed Rizzio over 50 times.

Little wonder she moved to the more secure lodging at Edinburgh Castle a few months later, when she gave birth to her son, the future James VI.

Above, from top.
Rizzio's murder depicted in a painting of the 1830s by Sir William Adam; Mary Queen of Scots' bedchamber at Holyrood; a portrait of Mary.

A ROYAL PARK

Part of Holyrood's appeal for the Stewart monarchs was its adjacent lands. These had once been part of the extensive estates of the abbey and were first enclosed by James V to form a royal park.

Although this was often referred to as a hunting park, there is little evidence that it was used for hunting deer during this period. They were occasionally brought to the Park from Falkland Palace in Fife, but this was unusual.

The court records suggest that when James enclosed the Park in 1541, his chief concern was the economic benefits. There are numerous references to sheep, cows and their associated by-products being used to provision the royal household.

Open-air activities

The recreational possibilities of the Park were not ignored completely, however. James V arranged hawking expeditions here for the entertainment of the court. He also held jousting tournaments here in 1527 and 1530.

At the marriage celebrations of Lord Fleming in 1562, Mary Queen of Scots held an outdoor masque in the Park. It is also said that she had a low-lying area of the Park flooded to provide a location for a miniature naval pageant, complete with replica boats.

Royal privilege

James V included lands around Duddingston in his enclosure, which was a blow to local residents, who had been accustomed to grazing their sheep there. Several cases were reported of tenants breaking down walls and building their own. To curb incursions, James V began appointing Park Keepers, who were responsible for maintaining a palisade or fence around the perimeter, and were granted accommodation within the Park.

By 1600, tenants were largely making use of the Park again. In 1610, James Ker, burgess of Edinburgh, petitioned the Privy Council for compensation after 80 of his sheep were killed here by dogs belonging to William Cuthbert, a butcher.

Efforts were still made to ensure royal use was not hampered. The grazing of livestock was forbidden in preparation for the visit of James VI in 1617 – aside from those beasts which belonged to the king and were being fattened up for his arrival.

Left. A jousting tournament in the late 1400s. Similar events were held by James V in Holyrood Park.

A DEBTORS' SANCTUARY

Below. An illustration of 1819 shows Holyrood Abbey at the right, the Palace at the centre and, at the left, St Ann's Yards, where debtors seeking sanctuary were lodged in tenements.

From at least the 1500s, the Park was a sanctuary, a place where a person could be safe from arrest or harm.

The right to sanctuary, known in Scotland as the 'privilege of girth', may date back to the 500s. It was often used by those fleeing arrest for serious crimes such as murder, but debtors also sought protection within the bounds of the sanctuary.

Holyrood was one of the largest sanctuaries in Scotland, taking in Arthur's Seat and stretching to the edge of Duddingston Loch. Records from the 1800s indicate debtors risked arrest if they went skating on the loch.

Holyrood provided a safe haven for debtors long after other sanctuaries had disappeared. It is not clear why. On entering the sanctuary, debtors were secure only if the appropriate fee was paid and recorded in the Register of Protections.

Between 1686 and 1880 (when the last debtor entered) there were 6,502 entries in the Holyrood register, suggesting the sanctuary was fairly well used. Sir Walter Scott's business partner Robert Caddell sought refuge here in 1826 when their publishing venture failed. Scott briefly contemplated it himself, writing, 'I suppose that I … will have to take up my residence in the Sanctuary for a week or so.'

AN AGE OF VIOLENCE AND CHANGE

Below. Illustrations of the Jacobite encampment in Holyrood Park, drawn from life in September 1745.

Murderous Muschat

A small cairn of stones stands near St Margaret's Loch, at the point where 17-year-old Margaret Hall was brutally murdered by her husband, Nicol Muschat.

On 17 October 1720, after several failed attempts on her life, the apprentice surgeon led her along Duke's Walk and slit her throat.

He was tried, found guilty, and sentenced to hang in the Grassmarket. Upon hearing of his 'unparalleled barbarity', his mother wrote to him, declaring, 'You have by your Wicked and Abominable Crimes, made me ashamed and sorry to own the Relation of Mother to you.'

SITTING PRETTY

Magdalen Pringle is thought to be the first person to write the word 'bonnie' when describing Prince Charles Stuart in one of her letters. The adjective stuck and is still used to this day.

All the prince's men

In September 1745, at the height of the last Jacobite Rising, Edinburgh was occupied by Prince Charles Edward Stuart and his supporters, who aimed to restore the Stuart dynasty to the throne.

Camping on the slopes of Arthur's Seat and in fields near Duddingston, the Jacobites kept out of range of Edinburgh Castle's guns. On 19 September, Charles held a council of war in a Duddingston tavern and resolved to advance on George II's army. He led his troops to victory two days later at the Battle of Prestonpans, having famously drawn his sword and thrown away the scabbard in a bold declaration of war.

For the following six weeks, the growing Jacobite forces camped in the Park. Here, Prince Charles would accustom them to the drills and orders of a regular army, prior to invading England.

This was the first time in six decades that Edinburgh had seen a royal prince, and Charles was met with much excitement. Magdalen Pringle, 18-year-old daughter of a Berwickshire laird, wrote of visiting the camp, where, 'He came out of the tent with a grace and majesty that is inexpressible.' However, she astutely predicted his later downfall: 'Poor man I wish that he may escape with his life. I have no notion that he'll succeed.'

An age of violence and change

Sound and vision

Just outside the Park is the site of a pioneering school for deaf children.

A blue plaque now marks the site once occupied by Thomas Braidwood's Academy for the Deaf and Dumb. Established in 1760, it was the first school of its type in the English-speaking world.

Here, through innovative teaching, students were taught to speak, lip-read and communicate through an early form of sign language. Many such pupils went on to achieve great success, including Francis Mackenzie, Lord Seaforth, Britain's first deaf Member of Parliament.

Nicknamed the 'Dumbie Hoose', the building was demolished in 1939, but gave its name to the area now known as Dumbiedykes.

Dissent in the ranks

In September 1778, Arthur's Seat was occupied during a military mutiny lasting three days and three nights.

The mutineers were 600 troops of the 78th Lord Seaforth's Highlanders. Rumours had spread that this newly formed regiment was to be sold to the East India Company, although the men had been recruited exclusively for home defence.

Their revolt became known as 'The Affair of the Wild Macraes', as many of the soldiers were of that name. They vowed to remain on Arthur's Seat until they received arrears pay, and assurance that they would not be sent to India.

These events caused quite a stir in Edinburgh. Sympathetic residents supplied the soldiers with food, water and music: Piper's Walk in the park is reputedly named after a local piper who played to buoy the Highlanders' spirits.

Their demands were eventually met after amicable negotiation. They were marched down to St Ann's Yards to receive the good news over bread, cheese and beer. The victory was, however, short-lived. Just three years later the entire regiment was dispatched to India. Many would never return to the Highlands.

Above left. The blue plaque marking Braidwood's Academy in Dumbiedykes.

Above right. A modern illustration of the Highlanders' revolt of 1778.

DISCOVERY AND PROGRESS

Up, up and away

Holyrood Park was witness to pioneering air travel by James 'Balloon' Tytler.

Tytler was described by Robert Burns as 'an unknown drunken mortal'. But in August 1784 this unlikely character became Britain's first aeronaut, flying from Abbeyhill, just north of the Park, for over half a mile, in a home-made hot-air balloon.

Tytler had researched ballooning while working on the *Encyclopaedia Britannica*, and set about designing and building his own. His prototype took shape beneath the partially-built dome of Register House on Princes Street. The admission fee charged to see it helped fund his full-sized balloon. His name survives in Tytler Gardens and Court, close to Holyrood Park.

Rock of ages

We now know that Salisbury Crags are composed of a sill of igneous rock, formed by cooling magma millions of years ago, but this knowledge is owed in no small part to an Edinburgh naturalist of the 1700s.

James Hutton laid the foundation for geological sciences, and he is credited as the 'Father of Modern Geology'. He based his theories on observations made while farming in Berwickshire, and during travels around Britain and Holland. But some of his key observations were made in Holyrood Park.

Hutton studied Salisbury Crags as they were revealed during quarrying, observing that an intrusion of molten rock had caused the Crags' formation. This was later used to prove that igneous rocks were the cooled forms of molten material from the interior of the Earth. The rock formation on which he focused is now known as 'Hutton's Section'.

Above. James Hutton depicted by the Edinburgh caricaturist John Kay.

In 1785 Hutton delivered his paper 'The Theory of the Earth' to the Royal Society of Edinburgh.

It contained a number of key ideas: that the Earth's core was hot, that the gradual weathering of rocks led to the formation of new continents on the sea floor, and that those processes shaping the Earth operated over an extremely long time.

This theory of Deep Time was controversial, since it challenged a widely accepted belief – derived from the Bible – that the Earth was no more than 6,000 years old.

Left. Tytler's Balloon, as illustrated on a handbill of the time.

Above. Hutton's Section seen in an illustration of the late 1700s, made by his friend John Clerk of Eldin.

A radical idea

Sir Walter Scott was behind one of Holyrood Park's most distinctive built features.

The base of Salisbury Crags was once skirted by only a rough track, providing access to the quarry faces above. In 1820, Scott was instrumental in providing a more formalised pathway for leisure and recreation.

Scott was familiar with Holyrood Park, having been educated nearby at the Royal High School. With a committee of friends, he arranged for the new road to be created by a group of unemployed weavers from the west of Scotland.

This early job-creation scheme came during the Industrial Revolution, when mechanisation was leaving many skilled craftspeople unemployed. An armed rebellion by workers in 1820, known as the 'Radical War', was harshly suppressed, but had caused alarm. This project was seen as a way to employ those who might otherwise be attracted to radical ideas.

The pathway they created became known as the Radical Road, and became the subject of a local riddle:

Round and Round the Radical Road
The Radical Rascal ran.
How many Rs are in that?
Tell me if you can.[†]

[†] The answer is none – no Rs in 'that'.

Top. The south side of Salisbury Crags, with Hutton's Section at the lower centre and the Radical Road above it leading up below the cliffs.

Above. Sir Walter Scott painted by Sir Henry Raeburn in 1822.

PLEASURE AND PROTEST

THE SKATING MINISTER

The subject of Henry Raeburn's famous portrait is thought to be his friend, Rev Robert Walker, minister of Canongate Kirk in the 1780s and 90s. Walker was a member of Edinburgh Skating Society, and is shown performing a challenging move at Duddingston Loch, where the skaters would often meet.

Right. Skaters on Duddingston Loch around 1900.

Far right. John Thomson's Tower, now inside Dr Neil's Garden, Duddingston; Frederick Douglass, the renowned American anti-slavery campaigner.

Frozen assets

When iced over, Duddingston Loch was a popular meeting place for winter sports.

The Edinburgh Skating Club, one of the oldest in Britain, used the loch to practise an early form of figure-skating, aiming to skate together in concert. Applicants for membership had to pass a series of tests, including jumping over a pile of hats three high.

The frozen loch also provided a good venue for the sport of curling and the Duddingston Curling Society was formed in 1795. Players of the game slide a specially polished stone across a sheet of ice, aiming for the centre of a target, while their partners brush the ice surface, helping steer the stone.

In 1804, Society members set down their rules for the game. Copies were printed and distributed, spreading quickly throughout Scotland. They were accepted as a national standard, and now form the basis of the international rules of curling.

Thomson and his tower

The Duddingston Curling Society needed a venue and enlisted the fashionable architect W.H. Playfair to design a new building, completed in 1825.

The octagonal tower takes its name from Rev John Thomson, minister of Duddingston Kirk, who used it as a studio where he could indulge his passion for painting.

He referred to the building as 'Edinburgh', so that his staff could inform visitors that the minister was unavailable, having 'gone to Edinburgh'.

The tower now sits within Dr Neil's Garden, a charming and secluded public garden next to Duddingston Loch (see page 55).

FATHER FIGURE

Rev Thomson is also said to be behind the popular Scottish saying, 'We're a' Jock Tamson's bairns.' There are other possible origins for this cheerful assurance that we all belong to one family, equal before God. However, it's tempting to relate it to Thomson: he was well loved for keeping his sermons short, and would often address his congregation as 'ma bairns'.

A grassroots movement

In April 1846, an influential visitor arrived in Edinburgh. Born into slavery in Maryland, USA, Frederick Douglass had escaped in 1838, and thereafter devoted his life to the abolitionist movement.

He had chosen a new name, inspired by the gallant Scottish knight Sir James Douglas in Walter Scott's poem *The Lady of the Lake*.

Douglass published his first autobiography in 1845 and, fearful of reprisals, came to Britain and Ireland, where he continued his campaign.

He settled for a while in Edinburgh, whose 'beauty, elegance and grandeur' he praised.

'Everything is different here,' he wrote. 'I am treated as ... an equal brother.'

He became known as an 'Anti-slavery agent', delivering hundreds of lectures around Scotland, on a circuit that had become well-established.

One target for his campaign was the Free Church of Scotland, which had accepted donations from slave-owners in the American south. Douglass and others adopted the slogan, 'Send back the money!'

On one occasion in May 1846, Douglass began to carve these words in large letters into the turf of Holyrood Park, though he was stopped before completing the task.

Decades later, Douglass returned to Edinburgh as an elderly man. He wrote of searching for his inscription, but discovering it had eroded to nothing.

BURIED SECRETS

In June 1836, five schoolboys were hunting for rabbits on Arthur's Seat when they discovered a small sealed cave on the slopes below the summit.

Inside were 17 miniature wooden coffins, arranged in three rows, each containing a little wooden figure. Each figure was carved and dressed as if to represent an actual person and the coffins were elaborately decorated with pieces of tin.

No clear explanation has emerged to account for these buried figurines. Some have suspected a black magic ritual; others have suggested they represent people who died at sea or abroad.

In the 1990s the coffins and figures were analysed in more detail. The fabrics worn by the dolls were found to date from the early 1830s – so they hadn't been buried for more than a few years when they were found.

This date ties in well with another theory: that they represented the 16 known victims of Burke and Hare, the notorious Edinburgh murderers. After selling the body of a deceased lodger named Davie for dissection, they turned to murder to provide further cadavers for the city's flourishing anatomy school. They were arrested in 1828. (Burke was convicted and hanged; Hare turned king's evidence and was spared.)

A more recent theory is that the figures are associated with the Radical War of 1820 (see page 25), after which three ringleaders were hanged and 20 of their followers transported to Australia. They were pardoned in 1835. The unemployed weavers who built the Radical Road may well have known the convicted men, and might have conceived these dolls as a secret tribute to them.

Eight of the miniature coffins and figures have survived, and are on display at the National Museum of Scotland.

Below. The miniature figures in their coffins.

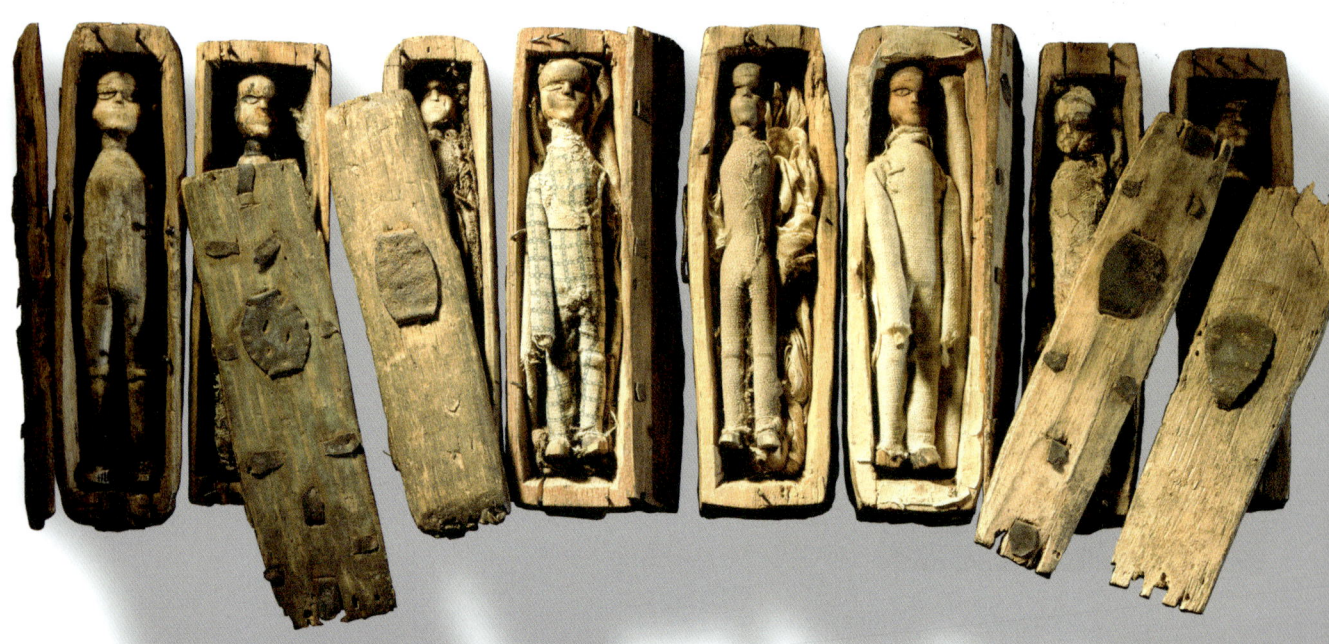

THE QUEEN'S PARK

It was Prince Albert, husband of Queen Victoria, who initiated the 'taming' of Holyrood Park for public recreational use.

When the royal couple first visited Holyrood in 1842 they found the Park largely a wilderness. The common sewers emptied out here and the land was marshy with a terrible smell.

In 1856, Albert put his ideas into action and the Park started to take on its current form. The Queen's Drive was built to allow exploration by carriage, the marshes were drained and St Margaret's Loch and Dunsapie Loch were both created. The flat ground between Holyrood and Meadowbank was converted from gardens and orchards into a flat area known as the Parade Ground.

The effects of Albert's actions can still be seen today. A number of Victorian buildings are still in use, including some of the five lodges built with the prince's support; and the Park is still primarily used for public recreation.

The Park's royal associations continue to this day. The Palace of Holyroodhouse is the King's official residence in Scotland and was for many years the venue for the late Queen's annual Garden Party.

Above. Victoria and Albert attending a military review.

Below. A contemporary illustration of the Volunteer Review held on 7 August 1860.

Review of the troops

In 1860, the Parade Ground was used for the Royal Volunteer Review, an elaborate military display with several regiments of the British Army taking part. Over 100,000 spectators attended, with some climbing the slopes of Salisbury Crags for a better view.

Similar events were held in later years, including the notorious 'Wet Review' of 1881, recorded with typical enthusiasm by the ungifted poet William McGonagall:

*'And to the Volunteers it was no lark,
Because they were ankle deep
in mud in the Queen's Park,
Which proved to the Queen
they were loyal and true,
To endure such hardships
at the Royal Review.'*

A STEP TOO FAR

Prince Albert wanted to transform the Park even further and had plans drawn up to build a thatched restaurant at Dunsapie. The plan met strong opposition, including several angry letters in *The Scotsman* newspaper, and was dropped.

IN PEACETIME AND IN WAR

A head for heights

Harold Raeburn was born into an Edinburgh brewing family in 1865, but soon turned his attention from beer to mountaineering. The Park provided a valuable training ground for him. The Park Regulations came into effect in 1872, restricting climbing to the South Quarry, so it was there that he learned his craft.

In 1896 Raeburn joined the Scottish Mountaineering Club, and within a few years he became its president. He recorded many classic climbing routes throughout Scotland.

Women were not permitted to join the club, so the Ladies' Scottish Climbing Club was formed in 1908. They practised on Salisbury Crags in full-length skirts, and were soon conquering Munros – Scottish mountains over 3,000ft (914m).

Climbing in the Park is still restricted to the South Quarry and climbers now require a permit. Please refer to our website for up-to-date information.

Target Edinburgh

During the First World War (1914–18), Holyrood Park was armed against the threat of invasion. Barbed wire, machine-gun posts and trenches were constructed to the south of Arthur's Seat, and practice trenches were built just north of Dunsapie. The defences were never needed against ground troops, but were put to the test on 2 April 1916.

At 7pm, two German Zeppelins were reported making their way towards the city. Street lights were lowered and traffic was stopped. Just before midnight, the first bombs fell on Leith. The bombardment continued for 30 minutes across the city. Thirteen people were killed, 24 were injured and many properties were damaged.

Four bombs hit Holyrood Park. Gunners on Arthur's Seat opened fire and eventually saw off the airships. This was the only air raid on Edinburgh during the war.

Top. An LZ-class Zeppelin, similar to the one that bombed Edinburgh in 1916.

Left top and centre. Harold Raeburn and a companion climbing Salisbury Crags.

A garden of one's own

During the First World War, 17 acres of Holyrood Park's parade grounds were set aside for use as garden allotments. This formed part of 200 acres across Edinburgh devoted to allotment cultivation when a U-boat blockade threatened to starve Britain into defeat. At Holyrood Park, allotment holders transformed what had been a 'dumping ground for refuse' into thriving garden plots.

After the war, the allotment lease on Holyrood Park was withdrawn. It was believed that 'Royal Parks maintained at public expense for the benefit of the people should be restored to their proper use'.

In the wake of the Second World War, however, the Parade Ground once again hosted allotments, which remained until at least the 1950s.

'By far the best thing for an unemployed man was to take up an allotment. It took him to the fresh air and to the country, and he could keep his family in vegetables for about six months of the year.'

Edinburgh Evening News
2 November 1933

Line of fire

For much of the 1800s and 1900s, Hunter's Bog was used for target practice by the army garrison based at Edinburgh Castle.

By the end of the 1800s, seven separate rifle ranges had been established, together with a small cluster of powder stores and pavilions. In later years they were used by volunteer brigades of the Royal Scots.

In 1896 the direction of the ranges was changed from north–south to west–east, across the valley. This was because residents in the nearby districts of Newington and Sciennes complained that bullets were reaching their houses and gardens.

The rifle ranges were used well into the 1950s, by the Territorial Army and civilians such as the Edinburgh Rifle Club. However, the targets and associated buildings were dismantled in 1961 and little remains of them now.

When the light is just right, platforms can be made out on the slope behind Salisbury Crags; while the locations of the buildings are indicated by low mounds. These features showed up quite clearly in recent laser scanning.

Below. This photograph of about 1846 shows members of the Edinburgh Castle garrison, among earliest users of the shooting ranges at Hunter's Bog.

PARK LIFE

The wool pack
Sheep once grazed freely throughout the valleys and crags of Holyrood Park – as many as 2,000 at one point. Their shepherds lived in lodges nearby.

Over time, the number of sheep declined. In 1977, as the Park was increasingly used by vehicles and dog-walkers, the sheep were finally removed.

Below. Eddie Sutherland, the last shepherd, photographed in 1977.

Their removal marked the end of the Park's long history as an agricultural landscape – only the cultivation terraces, lower rigs and some barely visible structures remain as a reminder of the days when Holyrood would ring with the sound of sheep and the calls of shepherds.

The last shepherd was Eddie Sutherland. He lived with his dog, Nap, in Wells o' Wearie cottage on the south side of the Park.

May Day dew
Climb to the top of Arthur's Seat on 1 May at dawn and you may witness an age-old tradition, as people wash their faces in the dew.

May Day marks the return of summer, and the fertility of the land. In ancient times, this was celebrated by the Gaelic festival of Beltane, at which great fires were kindled on hill-tops to honour the sun, protect cattle and encourage growth.

Water was considered sacred – it was vital to make things grow. May Day dew was viewed as the 'holy water' of the druids, guaranteeing vitality, beauty and good fortune for the year ahead.

By 1963, more than 1,000 people could be seen making the trek up Arthur's Seat at 5.18am (official sunrise time) to douse their faces with dew. The tradition still continues.

A recreational space

Close to the centre of Edinburgh, Holyrood Park remains a popular recreational space and is often the venue for major events. It has played host to the New Year's Day triathlon for over 20 years as well as a number of events including the Great Winter Run, the Great Edinburgh Run, Race for Life, Moonwalk Scotland, Run for Scotland, and the Rock'n'Roll Half Marathon.

The Park also provided the stage for the 102-mile bicycle road race at the 1970 Commonwealth Games. On a wet and windy day, the tough circuit around Arthur's Seat saw New Zealand's Bruce Biddle outsprint Australian Ray Bliney to win gold in 4 hours and 36 minutes.

Above. Fringe Sunday, held at the Park in August 1997; the Edinburgh Rock'n'Roll Half Marathon in August 2012; girls wash their faces in the dew on May Day 1959.

WHOSE SEAT IS IT ANYWAY?

This is not the only Arthur's Seat in Scotland. Ben Arthur, above Loch Long in Argyll, had the Gaelic name Suidhe Artair; and Suidhe in Glen Livet was known as Suiarthour: both of these names translate as 'Arthur's Seat'.

It is tempting to link such names to the legendary King Arthur, said to have led British resistance to Anglo-Saxon invasion in the 5th and 6th centuries. The colourful stories surrounding him have been associated with many locations, from Stirling and Meigle in Scotland to Tintagel in the far south-west of England.

However, there is little evidence to place him in Edinburgh. The earliest known use of 'Suidhe Artair' as a name for this hill is in a Gaelic poem of 1813.

An alternative theory suggests Arthur's Seat derives from the Gaelic *ard-na-said*, meaning 'height of the arrows', but this has been dismissed by Gaelic placename experts, who point to Scotland's other Arthur's Seats.

In 1503, long before any Gaelic name is recorded for the hill, it was already known as Arthurissete. The true origins of the name may never be known.

HOLYROOD PARK IN FICTION...

Holyrood Park has inspired many writers. Here are a few famous examples.

The Heart of Midlothian (1818)
Walter Scott
Published under the unlikely pseudonym of Jebediah Cleishbotham, this is widely considered the best of Scott's many 'Waverley novels'. It centres on Jeanie Deans, a dairy farmer's daughter, who walks from Edinburgh to London to petition the queen on behalf of her sister Effie, falsely convicted of infanticide. Jeanie lived at St Leonard's Bank, on the Park's south fringe. A cottage said to be hers survived until it was demolished in 1965.

The Private Memoirs and Confessions of a Justified Sinner (1824)
James Hogg
This is an audacious and unconventional novel, poised between gothic psychodrama and religious satire. It centres on two brothers, raised in different homes, whose conflicting personalities lead to violence and madness. A crucial confrontation between the brothers takes place at the summit of Arthur's Seat.

The Underground City (Les Indes Noires) (1877)
Jules Verne
The world's most translated French author, Verne visited Arthur's Seat in 1859. His mining mystery begins in Aberfoyle near Stirling but in one important episode the young heroine Nell, raised underground, is brought to Arthur's Seat to witness her first sunrise.

The Falls (2001)
Ian Rankin
Holyrood Park appears in several of Rankin's crime novels featuring Edinburgh detective John Rebus. In *The Falls*, the notorious miniature coffins found at Arthur's Seat provide Rebus with a lead as he investigates the disappearance of a banker's daughter during an online roleplay game.

Below left. Title page illustration from a French edition of *The Heart of Midlothian*.

Below right. Sharon Small and Ken Stott in the ITV adaptation of *The Falls*.

... AND ON FILM

Never mind Hollywood.
This is Holyrood.

Chariots of Fire (1981)
The multiple-Oscar-winning true story of two rival athletes at the 1924 Olympics stars Ian Charleson as Eric Liddell, a devout Scottish Christian. He is seen in one scene walking in Holyrood Park with his sister.

Adventures of Greyfriars Bobby (2005)
Edinburgh's canine celebrity famously guarded his late master's grave for 14 years until his own death in 1872. He is remembered in books, films and an A-listed statue. This version features scenes set in Holyrood Park. Despite a starry human cast led by James Cosmo, it provoked outrage by casting a West Highland terrier as Bobby, who was of course a Skye terrier.

The Illusionist (2010)
Sylvain Chomet moved to Edinburgh to make this melancholic animation, based on a script by French comedian Jacques Tati. Set in 1959, it focuses on a Parisian stage magician who travels to Britain seeking work, acquires a surrogate daughter in the Highlands and settles with her in Edinburgh. The city in the late 1950s is lovingly evoked, with two scenes set in Holyrood Park.

One Day (2011)
In David Nicholls' adaptation of his own novel, Anne Hathaway and Jim Sturgess star as Edinburgh University students who sleep together on 15 July 1988, the night of their graduation.

It charts their lives over 20 years, repeatedly revisiting them on the same date. Arthur's Seat features in scenes at the beginning and end of the story.

Trainspotting: T2 (2017)
Danny Boyle's film adaptation of Irvine Welsh's debut novel *Trainspotting* was released in 1996 to great acclaim and box office success. He reassembled the original screenwriter and cast for this much-deferred sequel. In one scene, reformed heroin addict Mark Renton (Ewan McGregor) drags his unreformed old pal Spud Murphy (Ewen Bremner) out for some exercise in Holyrood Park. The pair stop to rest at the summit of Arthur's Seat.

Top right. Anne Hathaway and Jim Sturgess in *One Day*.

Right. Ewan McGregor and Ewen Bremner in *Trainspotting: T2*.

EXPLORE HOLYROOD PARK

Holyrood Park is a beautiful, rugged space where you can see many species of wildlife, explore geological features and historic sites and enjoy fantastic views of Edinburgh and the landscapes surrounding the city.

In the pages that follow you can read about the Park's unique natural history, and the built environment that sheds light on human activity here over many centuries.

Please don't forget that the Park's wildlife habitats, geology and archaeological remains are vulnerable and already deteriorating. For example, skylarks were abundant, but are now rarely seen in the Park. We ask that you keep to the paths marked on the map (pages 2–3) and keep dogs on a leash or under close control.

Remember that the Ranger Service is available to help and advise you.

Below. The South Quarry, near the foot of Salisbury Crags.

A YEAR-ROUND WILDLIFE HABITAT

There are beautiful and unusual species to admire in every season. Featured on the next few pages are some of the particular highlights and rarities.

Spring

As the Park awakens from winter, temperatures rise, daylight lengthens and many plants and animals start to stir.

Many plants come into leaf, with some flowering early. Blackthorn, coltsfoot and cuckooflower add splashes of colour. By May, the gorse is a sea of deep yellow.

Toads rouse from hibernation and make their way to their ancestral spawning grounds. Thousands converge on Dunsapie Loch from the surrounding slopes.

Insects start to emerge, among them queen bumblebees, buzzing around for food and a suitable place to start a new nest.

Visiting birds such as willow warblers arrive in Scotland to nest. Their bright songs adds to the choir of birds already here and eager to establish territories and find a mate.

Summer

As the days grow longer and warmer, there is an explosion of wildlife that can be appreciated by all the senses.

Wildflowers bloom in a pageant of colours and scents – among them lady's bedstraw, viper's bugloss, mountain thyme and bird's-foot trefoil. Grasses are transformed into a shifting sea of diverse and changing shades as they come into flower.

Insects flit around, among them butterflies and day-flying moths. Darting dragonflies and damselflies add bright colour and movement.

In the skies, visiting swifts, swallows and martins glide and swoop, feeding on the glut of insects. Once the day shift is over, this role is taken up by the many bats living and feeding in the Park.

Left. Toads making the most of spring.

Top. A narrow-bordered five-spot burnet moth brings a splash of brightness to the summer.

A year-round wildlife habitat

Right. Swans undaunted by icy conditions on St Margaret's Loch.

Autumn

As the Park begins to cool, colours change to reds, golds and copper, peppered with berries – orangey-red rowans and deep purple brambles.

Still at large are some butterflies such as peacock and red admiral. Other insects are reaching the end of their lives: haggard bees are still foraging for pollen and nectar.

Summer migrants begin to depart, and there is less birdsong in the air – but other migrants such as wheatears and sandpipers may stop off and geese fly over the Park, heading south at the end of the growing season.

As vegetation recedes, there is more chance of spotting small mammals, scurrying as they search for food – or try to avoid becoming food!

Winter

Cold weather can be hard on the Park's wildlife, especially periods of snow on the ground and ice on the lochs.

Winter visitors such as redwings find some refuge around the Park. The numbers and variety of wildfowl swell with additions of goldeneye, wigeon, geese and sometimes even whooper swans.

Predators such as foxes, buzzards and kestrels have to work extra hard to find food and take advantage of opportunities when they occur.

As the winter draws to an end, birds begin their courtship behaviours. Swans dance; herons return to their heronry (nest colony); ravens swoop, play and display. These are all signs that spring is just around the corner.

Left. Foxes need to work harder when winter sets in.

Below. A tufted duck, one of the winter residents of St Margaret's Loch.

MEADOW AND GRASSLAND PLANTS

The meadows and heaths of the Park support a rich ecosystem. It is home to many interesting species not commonly found in the middle of a city.

FIND THE MAIDEN

Maiden pink

👁 Haggis Knowe | Early – midsummer
The beautiful maiden pink was at risk of local extinction until its recent revival in the Park.

The earliest record of maiden pink in the Edinburgh area comes from an unpublished manuscript of 1792. Isolated local populations have been identified over the years, but only a few are thought to remain.

This plant is recognised in the Edinburgh Local Biodiversity Action Plan, which works with organisations and individuals to conserve our wildlife. In 2013, the Royal Botanic Garden and City Council helped the Park conservation team plant maiden pink at five sites around Holyrood Park. This has now been propagated to some other parts of the city where it is known to have grown.

Lady's bedstraw

● On grassy slopes | Summer
White-flowered heath bedstraw and its yellow cousin lady's bedstraw are grassland plants producing a cloud of delicate flowers. Both grow throughout the Park. The yellow variety was once used to dye cloth.

Bird's-foot trefoil

● On grassy slopes | Summer
This plant was used both for yellow dye and as a treatment for eye infections. It is an important nectar source for many insects and a food plant for many larvae found in the Park.

Meadow and grassland plants

Harebell

- On grassy slopes | Summer – autumn

This iconic, deep blue flower is sometimes known as 'the Scottish bluebell'. Indeed, it closely resembles the bluebell, to which it is related.

Red campion

- On grassy slopes | Early – midsummer

This favourite food for bumblebees and butterflies goes by many names, including adders' flower, jack-by-the-hedge, red mintchop, soldiers' button and scalded apple. Its pretty, bright-red flowers close at night.

Thyme

- On grassy slopes | Summer

This aromatic herb grows widely in the Park. Widely used in cooking, it is also immortalised in the song 'Wild Mountain Thyme', written in 1948 by the Ulster piper Francis McPeake 1st.

Heather

- On grassy slopes | All year

One of Scotland's most widespread plants, heather has been used for many purposes, including thatching and brewing. It was also once a vital fodder crop: in snowy conditions, when grass was buried, shepherds brought their sheep to the Park's hilltops, where the wind exposed the heather shoots.

Sneezewort

- On grassy slopes | Summer

Until about 200 years ago, sneezewort was used as a common medicinal herb. Its advocates used it for promoting sneezing, both in people and animals. The root was also used to alleviate toothache.

Tormentil

- On grassy slopes | Summer

A small, pretty, yellow-flowered plant, tormentil has roots rich in tannin – a chemical with many uses, including tanning leather, brewing and winemaking: the bitter chemical helps keep alcoholic drinks fresh.

ROCK AND SCREE PLANTS

The Park's dramatic crags and rock-strewn slopes provide many different and challenging habitats. The plants that thrive here are adapted to these demanding conditions.

STUCK ON YOU

Sticky catchfly

👁 Samson's Ribs | Summer

Sticky catchfly has a beautiful flower that lights up the rock ledges where it is found.

This nationally rare plant was first discovered here in the Park, in 1668, by Thomas Willisel, official collector for the Royal Society of London. Its survival at Samson's Ribs, where it was first found, is almost miraculous. Elsewhere, populations have been lost to collecting, rock-falls, quarrying and fire.

The lower stems produce a sticky secretion. This is believed to be a defence against nectar and pollen-robbing insects, which bite holes in the base of the flowers. Small insects are often found stuck to the stem, giving the plant its name.

It is, however, an important food plant for butterflies, bees and hoverflies, which pollinate the flowers.

In recent years, the Park conservation team has worked with the Royal Botanical Garden Edinburgh to collect seeds from the few surviving specimens. The resulting plants have been planted in suitable locations throughout the Park and the Lothians to ensure its survival.

Gorse

• Throughout the Park | All year

The rich yellow undergrowth visible on many slopes in the Park is gorse, a member of the pea family with a distinctive coconut scent. It was traditionally used, beaten or ground, for animal fodder. It was said an acre of gorse could feed six horses for four months; and livestock that ate it in winter would never catch cold. It has also been used for dyes, firewood, chimney sweeping, drain filling, roofing, fencing, harrowing and foundations for paths and roads. Its ash was used as lye for cleaning linen.

Rock and scree plants

Rock whitebeam

- On rocks and cliff faces | All year

This rare tree has evolved to live on shallow rocky soils and cliffs where other trees cannot thrive. Historically the Park was heavily grazed by sheep, but whitebeam has survived by growing on inaccessible rock faces.

Spring sandwort

- On rocky outcrops | Late spring

This plant has a delicate appearance that can look somewhat out of place in the rugged environments where it grows in the Park. Its ability to grow in difficult conditions means it is a rare survivor.

Viper's bugloss

- Beside paths and tracks | Summer

A showy wildflower of dry banks, often seen on shallow soils. The name comes from its serpentine appearance, which led people to believe it could be used to treat snake bites. It can irritate the skin.

AQUATIC PLANTS

Aside from its three freshwater lochs, the Park has ponds, wet grasslands and marshy ground, all of which provide habitats for interesting, and in some cases rare aquatic plants.

1 Adder's tongue fern

• Hunter's Bog | Late spring/summer

This rare and unusual plant grows in old wet grasslands. It usually appears in summer, spending the rest of the year as a rhizome or underground stem. It tends to indicate the presence of ancient meadowland.

2 Common spotted orchid / 3 Northern marsh orchid

• Hunter's Bog | Late spring/summer

These beautiful flowers like wet, undisturbed grassland and are relatively rare. Their flowers are white, pink or pale purple with vivid deep purple patterns.

4 Horsetail

• Hunter's Bog | Spring – autumn

This plant appears in the fossil record from 150 million years ago and has changed little over the intervening years. It is rare now, but was once much more abundant. Horsetail has been used as a medicinal plant since Roman times.

5 Reedmace

• All lochs in the Park | All year

This reed was used for roofing, and was said to be highly resistant to vermin. It was also used by weavers to make part of their looms. The Statistical Account of 1796 records five acres of reedmace growing in Duddingston Loch.

6 Willow

• All lochs in the Park | All year

Parts of the willow have been used since prehistoric times. The sap contains a painkiller similar to aspirin, and the bark fibres make excellent twine. Felled when young, willow regrows readily, giving a regular supply of long straight poles. These were used for firewood, and to make tools and fences.

INVERTEBRATES

Don't forget to look out for insects and other invertebrates – a small but very important part of the Park's ecosystem.

BACK FROM THE BRINK

Northern brown argus butterfly

👁 High Road | Summer

Once commonly found in the Park, the northern brown argus butterfly was for many years thought to be extinct, but has recently re-appeared.

It is dependent on rockrose, a plant with bright yellow flowers that thrives on the thin, chalky soils on the Park's eastern slopes. When the road to Duddingston was built, rockrose was largely removed.

The northern brown argus was also widely collected by Victorian butterfly enthusiasts. Its re-establishment has been enabled by recent efforts to protect rockrose.

Other invertebrates

• All over the Park | Spring – autumn

The Park's rich and diverse plant life supports a wide variety of invertebrates. There are many moths and bumblebees **7**, and 11 species of butterfly are commonly seen. Aside from the northern brown argus (see left), look out for the peacock butterfly **8**. Its wings have large spots that look like eyes, repelling predators.

Another remarkable insect is the six-spot burnet moth, its bright red wing spots a warning to birds that it is toxic and not for eating. Also look out for the striking azure damselfly **9**, found seeking insect prey near the lochs.

MAMMALS AND AMPHIBIANS

A variety of mammals and amphibians can be found in the Park, if you look in the right places at the right times.

1 Bat

• Wooded areas/near water | Summer

Eight species of bat live in the Park. Natterers and brown long-eared bats feed in the trees around the perimeter. The three lochs are a favourite haunt of Daubenton's bat, which has exceptional echolocation, allowing it to fly very low, plucking insects off the water surface. Three species of pipistrelle, Scotland's smallest bats, are found throughout the Park. Lily Hill is a good place to spot bats at dusk.

2 Roe deer

• Murder Acre | All year

Roe deer have lived in Scotland since prehistoric times. They prefer woodland but can be seen grazing in the Park early in the morning, especially in winter time.

Much smaller than their cousin the red deer, they live alone except for mating or in very bad weather. Numbers were dropping but are now healthier.

SUBMERGING TALENT

Otter

• Duddingston Loch | All year

Once a rare species, the playful otter can now often be seen around Scottish waterways.

Historically the otter was hunted widely, for its soft waterproof fur, and to preserve fish stocks for anglers.

During the 1960s widespread use of toxic insecticides further reduced numbers. The otter is now legally protected and numbers have increased greatly.

This agile mammal feeds mainly on fish. Its thick pelt traps air for warmth and buoyancy. It swims well and can hold its breath for long periods.

BIRDS

3 Toad

The Park provides different habitats for a variety of birds. Many are resident all year while others come and go with the seasons.

- Dunsapie Loch / surrounds | April

Due to its warty skin, the toad has been unfairly associated with witchcraft and considered venomous. A toad does in fact secrete a toxin to deter predators. Dogs can foam at the mouth as a result of eating toads, but suffer no long-term effects. It was once believed that they had medicinal powers: rubbing a toad on an afflicted area was thought to draw out poisons and relieve sprains.

Every spring, many common toads are found on the High Road as they migrate from Arthur's Seat (where they hibernate) to their spawning grounds in Dunsapie Loch. The Ranger Service, with the help of local volunteers and the local conservation group LARG, help any stranded toads by keeping the road closed to traffic until they can be collected, counted and released into the Loch.

POISED TO STRIKE

Kestrel

- All over the Park | All year

The agile kestrel is a member of the falcon family, known for its ability to hover while searching for prey on the ground.

A true master of flight, it can be spotted hovering in all weathers, and always pointing head-first into any wind.

Its preferred prey are the voles and shrews that live throughout the Park's grassland, but it also eats insects, amphibians and small birds.

As well as superior flight skills, evolution has equipped the kestrel with the ability to see into the ultra-violet part of the spectrum. This helps it track prey by highlighting urine trails.

BIRDS
Continued

1 Fulmar

● Salisbury Crags | All year

The seagull-like birds on Salisbury Crags are fulmars – not gulls but a type of petrel. This is a true ocean-going bird: it even has a tube-like structure on its beak, enabling it to drink sea water by filtering out the salt. The name comes from Ancient Norse and translates as 'foul gull'. The fulmar spits the oily contents of its stomach at attackers. This sticky, smelly substance is notoriously hard to clean off and can remain on clothing for years. It can disable birds of prey, sticking to their flight feathers and leaving them unable to catch prey.

2 Heron

● All lochs in the Park | All year

Herons thrive in the Park, and can often be seen stealthily waiting and watching for a fish to swim through the shallow waters of Duddingston Loch. In springtime, their giant nests are visible, built on spindly trees. Herons pair for life and return to the same nest each year, making it bigger and bigger.

3 Kingfisher

● Duddingston Loch | All year

This tiny bird with vivid-coloured plumage is very shy, but with patience it can be spotted around Duddingston Loch. It nests underground in a deep tunnel that it builds for its young. Parents become muddy from crawling up and down the tunnel, so on leaving the nest they often dive into the water to clean their feathers.

4 Mute swan

● St Margaret's Loch | All year

The graceful water birds living on St Margaret's Loch are said to have been introduced by the Duke of Lauderdale in the 1670s. The king at that time was Charles II, who enlarged Holyrood Palace. He liked to serve swan at banquets, re-dressed in its feathers with a gilded beak.

Birds 49

6 Raven

- Raven's Rock / Craggy areas | All year

This is one of the Park's largest birds, with a wingspan of about 120cm. Its call is an unmistakeable croak. Like all crows, it is very intelligent and adaptable, and enjoys a varied diet of berries, nuts and carrion. Ravens were often seen feeding on dead lambs, which they were assumed to have killed. This led to their persecution, but in recent years they have made a welcome return, nesting on the Crags.

8 Skylark

- Grasslands | All year

This high-flying bird is not easy to spot but can sometimes be seen perched on a bush, often sporting a distinctive crest. It can be identified by its iconic song, a continuous lilting trill.

9 Swift

- All over the Park | Spring – summer

The swift arrives around May and is a harbinger of summer. After overwintering in Africa, it nests here and can be seen flying low over grassland and water, hunting for insects. Swifts never touch the ground – they even sleep on the wing.

5 Pheasant

- Throughout the Park | All year

The pheasant is not indigenous to Scotland but was introduced long ago, largely as a game bird. The male has a dark emerald head with scarlet skin around the eyes and long tail feathers. The female has plainer chestnut-coloured plumage.

7 Short-eared owl

- Whinny Hill / Hunter's Bog | Winter

Unlike other owls, the short-eared variety prefers to hunt during the day, flying low over rough grass and scrub looking for its prey. Some individuals have travelled to the Park from Scandinavia or even Siberia. They hunt voles, mice and shrews.

10 Wheatear

- Summit / Crags | Spring and autumn

This cheerful little bird can be identified by its distinctive white rump when it is disturbed and flies away. From this came its original name, 'white arse', changed to the more decorous modern name in Victorian times.

HISTORIC BUILDINGS AND STRUCTURES: HOLYROOD ABBEY AND PALACE

Intimately linked with the Park are the remains of Holyrood Abbey and the grand royal residence of the Palace of Holyroodhouse.

The abbey was founded in 1128 by King David I, supposedly to express his gratitude for a miraculous escape from death (see page 16).

Little is left of the original church except for a fine Romanesque processional doorway, which can be seen in the south wall.

Major rebuilding in the 1400s gave the abbey the plan it has today, although the only part now surviving is the nave – the western part of the church, where ordinary people worshipped.

The western façade is the undoubted highlight. It has been described as one of the most imaginative pieces of ecclesiastical architecture in Britain, although some of its symmetry was lost when the southern tower was demolished during the extension of the palace in the early 1600s.

The abbey had also been ransacked in 1544 and 1547, a victim of the English military campaign to force a marriage between Mary Queen of Scots and Prince Edward, later Edward VI of England.

The church reformed

In 1559 a Protestant mob attacked the abbey church, destroying its altars. The Reformation that followed in 1560 radically changed religious practice in Scotland. After this the abbey largely fell from use and in 1570 the choir, crossing and transepts were demolished. Visitors can still see the outline of these in the gardens to the east of the abbey.

The nave survived by being transformed into the Canongate parish church: the east wall was built at this time.

The decorative tracery in the east window was installed in 1633 for the Scottish coronation of Charles I.

The abbey has been a place of burial for several Scottish kings and members of the royal family. A Royal Vault was established in the south aisle and those interred include David II (1371), James II (1460), Madeleine de Valois (first wife of James V, 1537) and James V (1543).

Above. Holyrood Abbey.

Historic buildings and structures

Left. The fountain outside the palace, dating from around 1859 but modelled on Linlithgow Palace's fountain of the 1530s.

Bottom left. The Palace of Holyroodhouse.

The king's house

Holyrood Abbey was in use as a royal residence by the 1400s, with the surrounds of the royal park offering a more stately setting than Edinburgh Castle.

A new palace was constructed next to the abbey by James IV in the early 1500s, and it has remained an official residence of monarchs in Scotland ever since. It was used extensively by James V and was the main home of Mary Queen of Scots throughout her personal reign (1561–7).

Later developments

The quadrangle layout of the palace as it stands today dates to the 1670s, commissioned by Charles II and designed by the architect Sir William Bruce. For a long time, it housed members of the nobility in grace-and-favour apartments.

The palace was extensively modernised by King George V and Queen Mary in 1911–20.

Holyrood Abbey and Palace sit just outside the boundary of the Park. Note that the palace is not managed by Historic Environment Scotland. Ticketed admission and tours are managed by the Royal Collection Trust.

HISTORIC BUILDINGS AND STRUCTURES: IN AND AROUND THE PARK

Architectural features around the Park point to some of the many ways it has been used over the centuries.

St Anthony's Chapel
This dramatic ruin, perched on a rocky outcrop overlooking St Margaret's Loch, is the most prominent building within the Park.

Above left. St Anthony's Chapel as it may have looked when in use.

Above right. The surviving ruin of the chapel, viewed from a similar angle.

Although Holyrood Abbey controlled much of the Park, St Anthony's Chapel was a dependency of Kelso Abbey in the Scottish Borders. It was built at some point in the late-medieval period, and there is documentary evidence that it needed repairs in 1426.

The chapel is constructed from three types of stone – sandstone, basalt and tuff. While this gives it an attractive appearance, when it was in use the stonework was probably concealed under a layer of harling, a tough exterior plaster.

During the 1400s it became a popular place of pilgrimage, particularly on St Anthony's Day (17 January), Good Friday and the Exaltation of the Holy Rood (14 September). Easter visitors included James III and James VI, who donated a decorative frontal for the altar.

Not far below the chapel is one of the Park's holy wells, most of which have now disappeared. Its spot is marked by a boulder and a well-preserved stone bowl. It was probably in use around the same time as the chapel, though it could have earlier origins.

Historic buildings and structures

Left. A tunnel through which the Innocent Railway once ran.

Note that the Innocent Railway is just outside the Park boundary, and is not managed by Historic Environment Scotland.

Few records survive of the occupants of the cottages, though we do know that Eddie Sutherland, the Park's last shepherd, lived here (see page 32).

The Innocent Railway

The Edinburgh and Dalkeith railway was the city's first, and among the first in Scotland. Part of its line runs along the southern edge of the Park, and is now a walkway and cycle path.

The railway was opened in stages, beginning in 1831. It became known as 'The Innocent Railway' because its carriages were drawn by horses in an age when steam power was still considered dangerous.

It was used to transport coal from mines in the area around Dalkeith into Edinburgh, but soon also became popular with passengers. Around 300,000 people were carried annually, in open carriages, wagons and converted stagecoaches.

The railway had a terminus on the south side of Salisbury Crags. Entry into this terminus involved wagons being hauled through a sloping tunnel on a rope, operated by a steam engine. The tunnel still survives, as does a cast-iron beam bridge.

A branch line to Leith, to provide better access to the port, was opened in 1835.

The dam at Hunter's Bog

The monks of Holyrood Abbey made use of the Park's resources throughout the medieval period, farming its fertile lands and exploiting its water courses. At some point, the waters of Hunter's Bog were dammed at the northern end to power a mill.

The mill has now disappeared, but in the right light, the line of the dam is still visible on the ground. As well as powering the mill to grind grain, this water supply was also used for the monks' brewery, closer to the abbey. This began a long tradition of brewing in the area that continued until the 1980s.

Wells o' Wearie

A cottage known as the Wells o' Wearie stands on the south side of the Park. It dates back at least to the 1850s.

As the name suggests, there were once several wells in this area and they were used by local people to wash clothes. The clothes were bleached and then laid out to dry on the nearby slopes, although this practice was stopped in 1845 by crown commissioners who decried it as 'a nuisance of the most objectionable nature'. Today, the ponds at Wells o' Wearie provide important habitats for a diverse range of wildlife.

HISTORIC BUILDINGS AND STRUCTURES: DUDDINGSTON

Duddingston village occupies a picturesque location just outside the eastern edge of the Park, between Arthur's Seat and Duddingston Loch.

The Village
Made up mainly of cottages, Duddingston retains much of its traditional charm. The Sheep Heid Inn, near the centre of the village, dates from the 1300s and is one of Scotland's oldest pubs.

The village's attractive church was constructed around 1124. Like the rest of the village, it was built on land granted to Kelso Abbey by King David I.

Right. Duddingston Kirk.

Note that Duddingston Kirk, Duddingston Village and Dr Neil's Garden are just outside the Park boundary and are not managed by Historic Environment Scotland.

The original building consisted of a nave for ordinary worshippers, a choir for priests and a square tower. The original entrance, on the south side, is a round-topped doorway with particularly fine carving similar to the carving at Holyrood Abbey.

The church was enlarged by the addition of the Prestonfield Aisle in 1631. This additional space includes a gallery and burial vaults.

A gatehouse stands at the entrance to the kirkyard from the village. This was constructed in the early 1800s, as a lookout place to deter body-snatchers.

Some notable grave memorials survive in the picturesque kirkyard. The kirk is still in active use as a parish church of the Church of Scotland.

Once used for skating and curling, Duddingston Loch is now a wildlife reserve, supporting a diverse range of wildfowl and containing important reedbeds. It is managed by the Scottish Wildfowl Trust, who purchased the adjacent land at Bawsinch in 1971, extending the bird sanctuary.

Historic buildings and structures

Left. Thomson's Tower and Duddingston Kirk photographed from across the loch in the 1930s.

Below. Dr Neil's Garden.

Dr Neil's Garden

This garden is a tranquil space, located at the edge of Duddingston village, beside the loch. It's a perfect place to escape the hustle and bustle of the modern city.

The garden was created by Drs Nancy and Andrew Neil, a husband and wife team of general practitioners with a love of collecting plants from around Europe.

They began work on the garden in 1963 on an area once used for grazing, and the result is a peaceful and attractive retreat.

Plantings include conifers, heathers, rhododendrons, azaleas and magnolias, along with herbaceous borders. Following the death of the garden's creators in 2005, part of it was set aside as a physic garden as a special memorial to them, recognising their longstanding interests in horticulture and medicine.

Thomson's Tower

Set in a corner of Dr Neil's Garden, this unique, octagonal structure was designed by the renowned architect W.H. Playfair, a leading figure in Edinburgh's Enlightenment.

Built in 1825, the tower functioned as the meeting place of the Duddingston Curling Society – among the foremost exponents of the sport in the 1700s and 1800s, credited with writing the rules for the modern game. When it froze over, Duddingston Loch provided an ideal arena for the sport, which is believed to have originated in Scotland.

The tower has two storeys, each comprising a single room. The first-floor chamber would have been a comfortable space, with a fireplace and glazed windows. It was later used as a studio by the respected artist Rev John Thomson, minister of Duddingston, 1805–40.

The ground-floor chamber, with its floor only just above the water (or ice) level in the loch, was used for storing curling stones and other equipment. It was open to the elements so that the stones would remain at the right temperature. It now houses the Museum of Curling.

HELP US PROTECT THE PARK

We hope this book helps you enjoy your time in the Park and discover its extraordinary plants and animals, its long, eventful history and its important archaeological and geological features.

This precious and fragile area is a Scheduled Monument, and sensitivity is needed in its use and management. The Park has been in the care of public bodies since 1845. It is legally protected, in recognition of its important geology, wildlife and archaeological remains.

Today, Historic Environment Scotland is responsible for looking after the Park. Our Ranger Service and Conservation staff patrol it throughout the year.

However, we rely on the support of local users and visitors, and we ask you to follow the Holyrood Park Regulations.

To reduce erosion and disturbance to wildlife, we also ask walkers and runners to keep to the footpaths, and cyclists to use roads and cycle paths only. Note that access rights set out in the Scottish Outdoor Access Code do not apply in the Park.

For more information, please visit our website: historicenvironment.scot

Park rules in brief

For further information, please refer to the Park Regulations posted in the Park, or via the QR code opposite.

- Do not remove wildlife or geology from this protected area.

- Camping, lighting fires or barbecues, drone flying and off-road cycling are not allowed.

- Permission is required for events or gatherings in the Park.

- A permit is required for climbing or fishing. This can be obtained free of charge from the Ranger Service.

- Well behaved dogs are welcome in Holyrood, but dog owners must respect wildlife and other Park users.

- During the spring and summer it is essential to keep dogs on a short lead or close at heel. Ground-nesting birds and other animals are very vulnerable to disturbance.

- Any archaeological finds must be reported to the Ranger Service. Metal-detecting and digging are strictly prohibited.

- Please take all litter and dog waste home with you, or dispose of it in the bins provided.

Appropriate footwear is essential when exploring the steep and rugged terrain of Holyrood Park. Please also stick to the footpaths.

Please refer to our website for up-to-date information on any path and road closures in the Park.

Holyrood Park Rangers
0131 652 8150
rangers@hes.scot